Indiana Ecoregions

- Southern Michigan/Northern Indiana Drift Plains
- Interior River Valleys and Hills
- Eastern Corn Belt Plains
- Central Corn Belt Plains
- Huron/Erie Lake Plains
- Interior Plateau

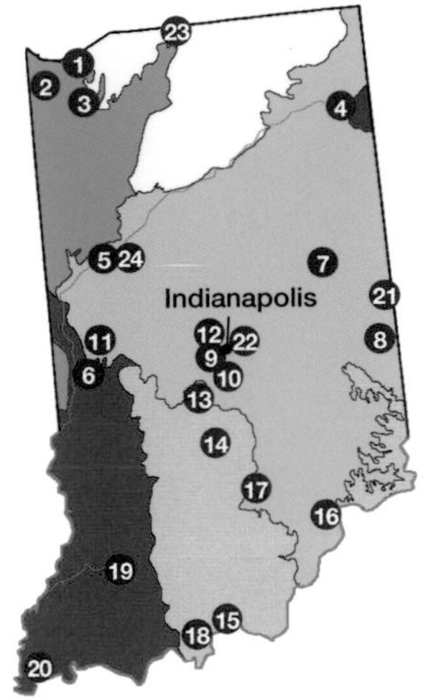

1. Indiana Dunes National Lakeshore
2. Hoosier Prairie Nature Preserve
3. Taltree Arboretum & Gardens
4. Bicentennial Woods Nature Preserve
5. Clegg Botanical Gardens
6. Turkey Run State Park
7. Christy Woods/ Ball State University
8. Lick Creek Summit Nature Preserve
9. White River Gardens
10. Holcomb Botanical Garden
11. Pine Hills Nature Preserve/ Shades State Park
12. Nature Center at Eagle Creek Park
13. Morgan-Monroe State Forest
14. Yellowwood State Forest/ Brown County State Park
15. O'Bannon Woods Interpretive Center
16. Clifty Falls State Park
17. Jackson-Washington State Forest
18. Hoosier National Forest
19. Thousand Acre Woods State Nature Preserve
20. Twin Swamps Nature Preserve
21. Hayes Arboretum
22. Garfield Park Conservatory & Sunken Gardens
23. South Bend Conservatories
24. Purdue University Horticultural Gardens

Measurements denote the height of plants unless otherwise indicated. Illustrations are not to scale.

N.B. – Many edible wild plants have poisonous mimics. Never eat a wild plant or fruit unless you are absolutely sure it is safe to do so. The publisher makes no representation or warranties with respect to the accuracy, completeness, correctness or usefulness of this information and specifically disclaims any implied warranties of fitness for a particular purpose. The advice, strategies and/or techniques contained herein may not be suitable for all individuals. The publisher shall not be responsible for any physical harm (up to and including death), loss of profit or other commercial damage. The publisher assumes no liability brought or instituted by individuals or organizations arising out of or relating in any way to the application and/or use of the information, advice and strategies contained herein.

Made in the USA

Waterford Press publishes reference guides that introduce readers to nature observation, outdoor recreation and survival skills. Product information is featured on the website: **www.waterfordpress.com**

Text & illustrations © 2008, 2024 Waterford Press Inc. All rights reserved. Photos © Shutterstock. Ecoregion map © The National Atlas of the United States.
To order or for information on custom published products, please call 800-434-2555 or email orderdesk@waterfordpress.com. For permissions or to share comments, email editor@waterfordpress.com.

ISBN 978-1-58355-447-0 $8.95 U.S.
9 781583 554470 50895
UPC 8 84682 01664 7
10 9 8 7 6 5 4 3 2 1 2400718

INDIANA TREES & WILDFLOWERS – A Folding Pocket Guide to Familiar Plants

WATERFORD PRESS

A POCKET NATURALIST® GUIDE

INDIANA TREES & WILDFLOWERS

A Folding Pocket Guide to Familiar Plants

T0123983

Eastern White Pine
Pinus strobus To 100 ft. (30 m)
Needles grow in bundles of 5. Cone is up to 8 in. (20 cm) long.

Eastern Hemlock
Tsuga canadensis To 150 ft. (45 m)
Flat needles grow from 2 sides of twigs, parallel to the ground. Tip of tree usually droops.

Eastern Red-cedar
Juniperus virginiana To 60 ft. (18 m)
4-sided branchlets are covered with overlapping, scale-like leaves. Fruit is a blue berry.

Eastern Cottonwood
Populus deltoides To 100 ft. (30 m)
Leaves are up to 7 in. (18 cm) long. Flowers are succeeded by capsules containing seeds with cottony "tails."

Trembling Aspen
Populus tremuloides To 70 ft. (21 m)
Long-stemmed leaves rustle in the slightest breeze. The most widely distributed tree in North America.

Bigtooth Aspen
Populus grandidentata To 60 ft. (18 m)
Leaves have large, blunt teeth along the edges. Flowers bloom in a long cluster.

Black Willow
Salix nigra To 100 ft. (30 m)
Tree or shrub, often leaning. Slender leaves are shiny green on the upper surface. Flowers bloom in long, fuzzy clusters.

Shagbark Hickory
Carya ovata To 100 ft. (30 m)
Bark curls away from the trunk, giving it a shaggy appearance. Leaves have 5 leaflets.

Black Walnut
Juglans nigra To 90 ft. (27 m)
Leaves have 9-23 leaflets. Greenish fruits have a black nut inside.

American Hornbeam
Carpinus caroliniana To 30 ft. (9 m)
Also called blue beech, it has blue-gray bark and a "muscular" trunk. Distinctive fruits have seeds contained in 3-sided bracts.

Eastern Hophornbeam
Ostrya virginiana To 50 ft. (15 m)
Trunk has sinewy, muscle-like bark. Hop-like fruits are hanging, cone-like clusters.

American Beech
Fagus grandifolia To 80 ft. (24 m)
Flowers bloom in rounded clusters in spring and are succeeded by 3-sided nuts.

White Oak
Quercus alba To 100 ft. (30 m)
Leaves have 5-9 rounded lobes. Acorn has a shallow, scaly cup.

Swamp White Oak
Quercus bicolor To 70 ft. (21 m)
Grows in lowlands and wet, flat areas. Leaves have rounded teeth. Acorns usually occur in pairs.

Chinkapin Oak
Quercus muehlenbergii To 80 ft. (24 m)
Leaves are up to 6 in. (15 cm) long and are coarsely-toothed.

Northern Red Oak
Quercus rubra To 90 ft. (27 m)
Large tree has a rounded crown. Leaves have 7-11 spiny lobes.

Black Oak
Quercus velutina To 80 ft. (24 m)
Leaves have 5-7 spiny lobes. Acorns have a ragged-edged cup.

Hackberry
Celtis occidentalis To 90 ft. (27 m)
Leaves are slightly toothed and curved at the tip. Red-to-purple fruits grow singly at the end of long stems.

American Elm
Ulmus americana To 100 ft. (30 m)
Note vase-shaped profile. Leaves are toothed. Fruits have a papery collar and are notched at the tip.

Sweetgum
Liquidambar styraciflua To 100 ft. (30 m)
Small, greenish flowers bloom in tight, round clusters and are succeeded by hard fruits covered with woody spines.

Red Mulberry
Morus rubra To 60 ft. (18 m)
Leaves are 3-lobed, oval or mitten-shaped. Elongate fruit is edible.

Tulip Tree
Liriodendron tulipifera To 120 ft. (36.5 m)
Note unusual leaf shape. Showy flowers are succeeded by cone-like aggregates of papery, winged seeds.
Indiana's state tree.

Sassafras
Sassafras albidum To 60 ft. (18 m)
Aromatic tree or shrub has variously shaped leaves. Fruits are dark berries.

American Sycamore
Platanus occidentalis To 100 ft. (30 m)
Leaves have 3-5 shallow lobes. Rounded fruits are bristly.

Hawthorn
Crataegus spp. To 40 ft. (12 m)
Tree has rounded crown of spiny branches. Apple-like fruits appear in summer.

Black Cherry
Prunus serotina To 80 ft. (24 m)
Aromatic bark and leaves smell cherry-like. Dark berries have an oval stone inside.

Eastern Redbud
Cercis canadensis To 40 ft. (12 m)
Showy magenta, pea-shaped flowers are succeeded by oblong seed pods.

Honey Locust
Gleditsia triacanthos To 80 ft. (24 m)
Leaves have 7-15 pairs of leaflets. Twisted fruits are up to 16 in. (40 cm) long.

Boxelder
Acer negundo To 60 ft. (18 m)
Leaves have 3-7 leaflets. Seeds are encased in paired papery keys.

Red Maple
Acer rubrum To 90 ft. (27 m)
Leaves have 3-5 lobes and turn scarlet in autumn. Flowers are succeeded by red, winged seed pairs.

Silver Maple
Acer saccharinum To 80 ft. (24 m)
Note short trunk and spreading crown. Five-lobed leaves are silvery beneath.

Sugar Maple
Acer saccharum To 100 ft. (30 m)
Leaves have 5 coarsely-toothed lobes. Fruit is a winged seed pair. Tree sap is the source of maple syrup.

American Basswood
Tilia americana To 100 ft. (30 m)
Leaves are heart-shaped. Flowers and nutlets hang from narrow leafy bracts.

Flowering Dogwood
Cornus florida To 30 ft. (9 m)
Tiny flowers bloom in crowded clusters surrounded by 4 white petal-like structures.

Black Tupelo
Nyssa sylvatica To 100 ft. (30 m)
Crown has horizontal branches. Glossy leaves turn red in autumn. Blue fruits have ridged seeds.

Green Ash
Fraxinus pennsylvanica To 60 ft. (18 m)
Leaves have 7-9 leaflets. Fruits are produced in winged clusters.

Pawpaw
Asimina triloba To 30 ft. (9 m)
Large leaves, to 12 in. (30 cm) long, turn yellow when fruits ripen. Oblong fruits blacken when ripe.

Eastern Burningbush
Euonymus atropurpureus To 20 ft. (6 m)
Red and purple flowers are succeeded by red and purple seeds.

Sandbar Willow
Salix exigua To 10 ft. (3 m)
Shrub forms thickets on wet soils.

American Bladdernut
Staphylea trifolia To 26 ft. (8 m)
Shrub or small tree has leaves with 3 leaflets. Flowers are succeeded by 3-part bladder-like fruits.

Elderberry
Sambucus spp. To 16 ft. (4.8 m)
Leaves have 5-7 leaflets and are sharply toothed.

Spicebush
Lindera benzoin To 17 ft. (5.1 m)
Shrub has small yellow flowers succeeded by bright red berries.

Smooth Sumac
Rhus glabra To 20 ft. (6 m)
Clusters of white flowers are succeeded by "hairy" red fruits. Bark is gray and smooth.

Blackhaw
Viburnum prunifolium To 20 ft. (6 m)
Clusters of white flowers are succeeded by dark, edible fruits.

New Jersey Tea
Ceanothus spp. To 4 ft. (1.2 m)
Leaves were used to make tea during the American Revolution.

Pussy Willow
Salix discolor To 20 ft. (6 m)
Distinctive fuzzy catkins appear in spring before the leaves.

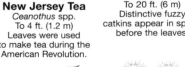

Common Serviceberry
Amelanchier arborea To 40 ft. (12 m)
White, star-shaped flowers bloom early in spring. Red to purple-black berries ripen in mid-summer.

Eastern Poison Ivy
Toxicodendron radicans To 8 ft. (2.4 m)
Flowers bloom in loose clusters. 3-part leaves turn red in autumn.

Buttonbush
Cephalanthus occidentalis To 10 ft. (3 m)
"Pincushion" flowers have protruding stamens.

Bloodroot
Sanguinaria canadensis
To 10 in. (25 cm)
Blooms in early spring.

Pussytoes
Antennaria spp.
To 16 in. (40 cm)
Woolly stalks support
fluffy flowerheads.

Oxeye Daisy
Leucanthemum vulgare
To 3 ft. (90 cm)
Showy flowers bloom
along roadsides
in summer.

Water Hemlock
Cicuta maculata
To 7 ft. (2.1 m)
Wetland plant has flat-
topped clusters of white
flowers and 2-3 lobed
leaves. All parts of the
plant are poisonous.

Queen Anne's Lace
Daucus carota
To 4 ft. (1.2 m)
Flower clusters become
cup-shaped as they age.

Large-flowered Trillium
Trillium grandiflorum
To 18 in. (45 cm)
3 white petals turn
pinkish with age.

Flower-of-an-hour
Hibiscus trionum
To 2 ft. (60 cm)

Boneset
Eupatorium perfoliatum
To 4 ft. (1.2 m)
Hairy plant with stout,
erect stem. Opposite
leaves are lance-shaped.
Fuzzy, white flowers
bloom in dense clusters.

Wild Strawberry
Fragaria spp.
Stems to 8 in. (20 cm)
Creeping plant has
5-petalled flowers
that are succeeded
by the familiar fruit.

White Sweet Clover
Melilotus albus
To 8 ft. (2.4 m)
Leafy plant has long
spikes of tiny, white
pea-shaped flowers.

Mayapple
Podophyllum peltatum
To 18 in. (45 cm)
Cup-shaped flowers
bloom between 2
leaves. Fruits are yellow.

Smooth Solomon's Seal
Polygonatum biflorum
To 7 ft. (2.1 m)
Hanging, bell-shaped
flowers are succeeded by
blackish fruits in fall.

Yarrow
Achillea millefolium
To 3 ft. (90 cm)
Leaves are fern-like.
Each tiny flower
has 4-6 rays.

Arrowhead
Sagittaria latifolia
To 4 ft. (1.2 m)
Aquatic plant has
arrow-shaped leaves.

Nodding Lady's Tresses
Spiranthes cernua
To 2 ft. (60 cm)
Flowers bloom
in spiral rows
on flower stalk.

Dutchman's Breeches
Dicentra cucullaria
To 12 in. (30 cm)
Spurred flowers
resemble trousers.

Butterfly Weed
Asclepias tuberosa
To 3 ft. (90 cm)
Orange flowers
are star-shaped.

Marsh Marigold
Caltha palustris
To 2 ft. (60 cm)
Aquatic plant has large,
heart-shaped leaves and
bright yellow flowers.

Common Sunflower
Helianthus annuus
To 13 ft. (3.9 m)
Flowers follow the sun
across the sky each day.

Michigan Lily
Lilium michiganense
To 5 ft. (1.5 m)

Common St. John's Wort
Hypericum spp.
To 30 in. (75 cm)
Widespread weed is
found in waste areas.

Butter-and-Eggs
Linaria vulgaris
To 3 ft. (90 cm)
Spurred flowers
have a patch of

Gray-headed Coneflower
Ratibida pinnata
To 5 ft. (1.5 m)

Common Evening Primrose
Oenothera biennis
To 5 ft. (1.5 m)
Lemon-scented,
4-petalled flowers
bloom in the evening.

Yellow Wood Sorrel
Oxalis stricta
To 15 in. (38 cm)
Leaves are clover-
like. Fruits look like
candlesticks.

Buttercup
Ranunculus spp.
To 3 ft. (90 cm)
Flower petals are
waxy to the touch.

Black-eyed Susan
Rudbeckia hirta
To 3 ft. (90 cm)
Flower has a dark,
conical central disk.

Orange Hawkweed
Hieracium spp.
To 2 ft. (60 cm)
Hairy plant has leaves
clustered at its base.

Goldenrod
Solidago spp.
To 5 ft. (1.5 m)
Flowers bloom in
arched clusters.

Downy Yellow Violet
Viola pubescens
To 16 in. (35 cm)

Trout Lily
Erythronium americanum
To 10 in. (25 cm)
Common in meadows and
rich woodlands.

Downy Yellow Foxglove
Aureolaria spp.
To 5 ft. (1.5 m)

Yellow Lady's Slipper
Cypripedium spp.
To 28 in. (70 cm)

Common Mullein
Verbascum thapsus
To 7 ft. (2.1 m)
Common
roadside weed.

Golden Alexanders
Zizia aurea
To 3 ft. (90 cm)
Small flowers bloom
in flat-topped clusters.

Shrubby Cinquefoil
Potentilla simplex
Sprawling roadside
plant has leaves
with 5 leaflets.

Hog Peanut
Amphicarpaea bracteata
Vine to 4 ft. (1.2 m)

Common Milkweed
Asclepias syriaca
To 6 ft. (1.8 m)
Pink-purple flowers bloom
in drooping clusters.

Wild Ginger
Asarum canadense
To 12 in. (30 cm)
Flowers arise at base
of 2 leaves.

Spring Beauty
Claytonia virginica
To 12 in. (30 cm)

Teasel
Dipsacus spp.
To 7 ft. (2.1 m)

Joe-Pye Weed
Eutrochium spp.
To 7 ft. (2.1 m)
Flowers are pink to
purple. Leaves grow in
whorls of 3-5.

Wild Geranium
Geranium maculatum
To 2 ft. (60 cm)

Cardinal Flower
Lobelia cardinalis
To 4 ft. (1.2 m)

Blazing Star
Liatris spp.
To 5 ft. (1.5 m)

Red Clover
Trifolium pratense
To 2 ft. (60 cm)
Leaves have
3 leaflets.

Phlox
Phlox spp.
To 20 in. (50 cm)
Five-petalled, yellow-
centered flowers may be
white, yellow, pink, red
or lavender. Grows in
sprawling clusters.

Peony
Paeonia spp.
To 2 ft. (60 cm)
Flowers are various
shades of pink and white.
Indiana's state flower.
It is not a native or
naturalized cultivar.

False Dragonhead
Physostegia virginiana
To 4 ft. (1.2 m)

Pasture Rose
Rosa carolina
To 3 ft. (90 cm)

Fire Pink
Silene virginica
To 2 ft. (60 cm)

Canada Thistle
Cirsium arvense
To 4 ft. (1.2 m)
Note deeply lobed oblong leaves
with spiny-toothed edges.

Corn Cockle
Agrostemma spp.
To 3 ft. (90 cm)

Queen-of-the-Prairie
Filipendula rubra
To 6 ft. (1.8 m)

Aster
Aster spp.
To 12 in. (30 cm)

Wild Mint
Mentha arvensis
To 31 in. (78 cm)
Lavender to white
flowers grow in
clusters at leaf bases.

Bluets
Houstonia spp.
To 6 in. (15 cm)
Yellow-centered flowers
grow in large colonies.

Beardtongue
Penstemon spp.
To 4 ft. (1.2 m)
Lower lip and throat
of flower is "bearded"
with fine hairs.

Passionflower
Passiflora incarnata
Climbing vine
to 20 ft. (6 m) high.

Great Blue Lobelia
Lobelia siphilitica
To 4 ft. (1.2 m)

Allegheny Monkeyflower
Mimulus ringens
To 3 ft. (90 cm)
Bluish, yellow-centered
flowers have a
puffy lower lip.

Bluebells
Mertensia spp.
To 30 in. (75 cm)

Beebalm
Monarda spp.
To 4 ft. (1.2 m)

Venus' Looking Glass
Triodanis perfoliata
To 2 ft. (60 cm)
Note how leaves
"clasp" the stem.

Spiderwort
Tradescantia spp.
To 3 ft. (90 cm)

Iris
Iris spp.
To 31 in. (78 cm)

Heal-all
Prunella vulgaris
To 12 in. (30 cm)
Opposite oval leaves are
lance-shaped. Blossoms
have a fringed lower lip.

True Forget-me-not
Myosotis scorpioides
To 2 ft. (60 cm)
Small sky-blue flowers
have yellow centers.

Morning Glory
Ipomoea spp.
Vine to 30 ft. (9 m)
Trumpet-shaped flowers
may be red, pink, blue,
white or purple.

Blue Vervain
Verbena hastata
To 6 ft. (1.8 m)
Has a slender spike
of bluish flowers.

Closed Gentian
Gentiana andrewsii
To 2 ft. (60 cm)

Common Blue Violet
Viola sororia
To 8 in. (20 cm)

Ironweed
Vernonia spp.
To 5 ft. (1.5 m)
Flowers are
thistle-like.